⬚ READERS

Level 1

Level 2

A Note to Parents

DK READERS is a compelling program for beginning readers, designed in conjunction with leading literacy experts, including Dr. Linda Gambrell, Professor of Education at Clemson University. Dr. Gambrell has served as President of the National Reading Conference and the College Reading Association, and has recently been elected to serve as President of the International Reading Association.

Beautiful illustrations and superb full-color photographs combine with engaging, easy-to-read stories and informational texts to offer a fresh approach to each subject in the series. Each DK READER is guaranteed to capture a child's interest while developing his or her reading skills, general knowledge, and love of reading.

The five levels of DK READERS are aimed at different reading abilities, enabling you to choose the books that are exactly right for your child:

Pre-level 1: Learning to read
Level 1: Beginning to read
Level 2: Beginning to read alone
Level 3: Reading alone
Level 4: Proficient readers

The "normal" age at which a child begins to read can be anywhere from three to eight years old. Adult participation through the lower levels is very helpful for providing encouragement, discussing storylines, and sounding out unfamiliar words.

No matter which level you select, you can be sure that you are helping your child learn to read, then read to learn!

LONDON, NEW YORK,
MELBOURNE, MUNICH, AND DELHI

Project Editor Laura Gilbert
Designer Jon Hall
Brand Manager Lisa Lanzarini
Publishing Manager Simon Beecroft
Category Publisher Siobhan Williamson
Production Nick Seston
DTP Designer Santosh Kumar G

Lucasfilm
Executive Editor Jonathan W. Rinzler
Art Director Troy Alders
Continuity Supervisor Leland Chee

Reading Consultant
Linda B. Gambrell, Ph.D.

First published in the United States in 2007
by DK Publishing,
375 Hudson Street
New York, New York 10014

10 11 10 9 8 7 6

SD354—8/07

A catalog record for this book is available from the Library of Congress.

ISBN: 978-0-7566-3274-8 (Paperback)
ISBN: 978-0-7566-3275-5 (Hardback)

Color reproduction by Wyndeham Pre-Press Ltd., UK
Printed and bound in China by L Rex Printing Co., Ltd.

Discover more at
www.dk.com

www.starwars.com

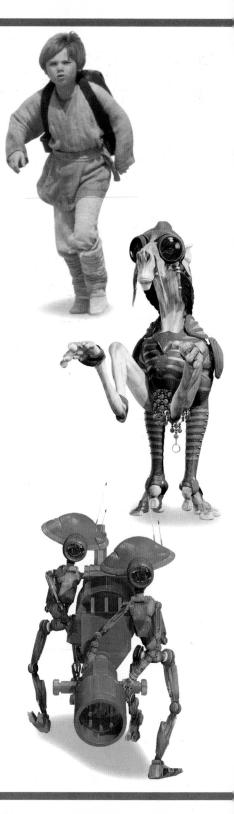

DK READERS

STAR WARS

READY, SET, PODRACE!

WITHDRAWN

BEGINNING **1** TO READ

Written by Simon Beecroft

Do you like fast races?

Would you like to see
the fastest race ever?

A Podrace is the fastest race
you will ever see!

In a Podrace, each pilot flies
a machine called a Podracer.

Podracers fly just above
the ground.

Podracers fly very fast!

Podracer

Podracer pilots sit
in a seat called
a cockpit.

Cockpit

All the driving controls
are in front of them.

The pilots have to move
the controls very quickly
when they are racing.

Do you think you could fly
a Podracer?

This desert racetrack has lots of
twists and turns.
Some of these twists and turns
are very dangerous.

The pilot who
reaches the end
of the race first
is the winner.

Racetrack

Many people come to watch
the Podraces.
The people shout and cheer.

They are excited to see the race.
They want to find out
which racer will win.

Podracing is very dangerous.

The pilots fly along at really
fast speeds.

Some racers crash into each other, and some racers crash into cliffs.

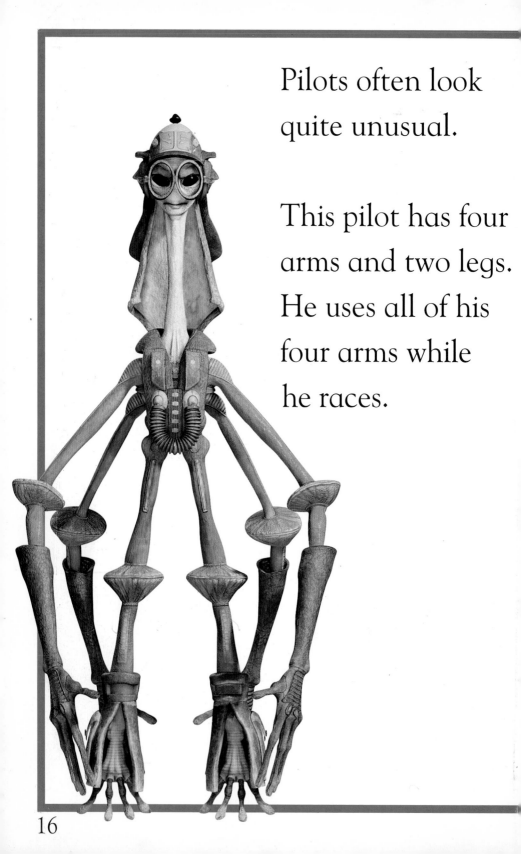

Pilots often look
quite unusual.

This pilot has four
arms and two legs.
He uses all of his
four arms while
he races.

This pilot has three eyes.
His extra eye helps him
spot dangers in the race.

This pilot is wearing goggles.
They are special racing goggles.
His racing goggles
protect his eyes
from the desert sand.

This pilot is nervous.
He is worried because
his Podracer is broken.
He will not finish the race.

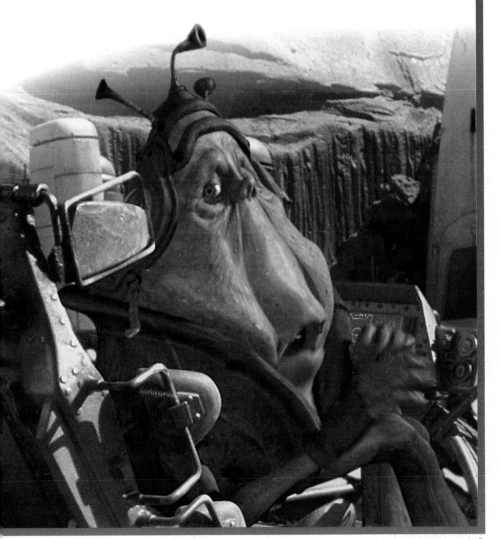

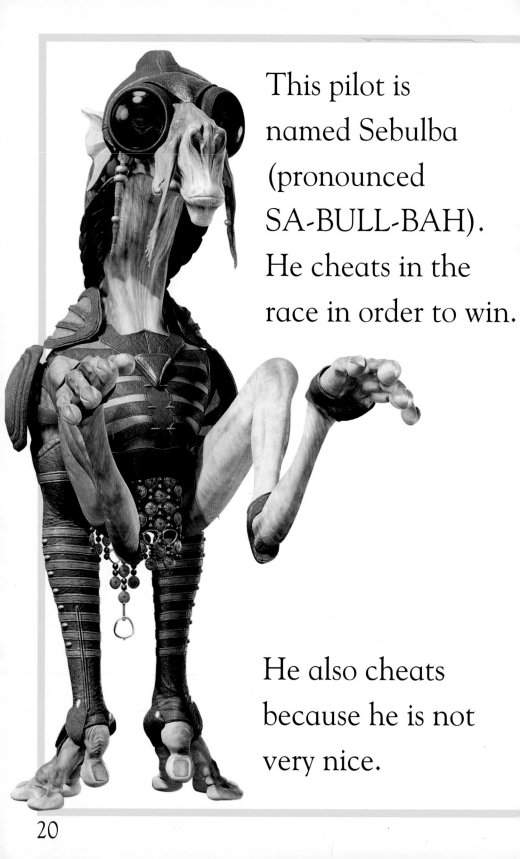

This pilot is
named Sebulba
(pronounced
SA-BULL-BAH).
He cheats in the
race in order to win.

He also cheats
because he is not
very nice.

Robots clean
the Podracers and
repair the engines.

Each pilot makes
sure his Podracer
is ready to go!

Engines

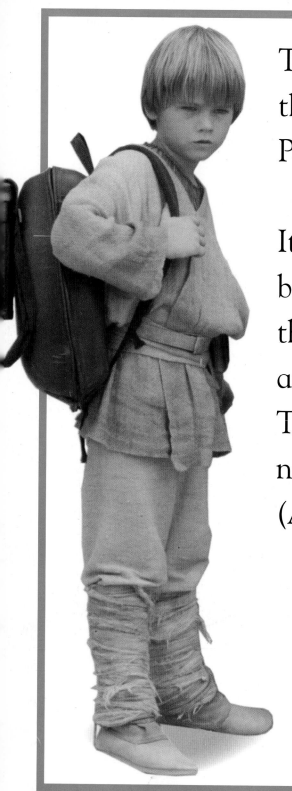

Today is one of the most exciting Podraces ever.

It is exciting because one of the racers is a young boy. The boy is named Anakin (AN-NA-KIN).

Anakin has never finished
a Podrace before.

Anakin built his Podracer all
by himself.

He is only nine years old,
but he is a very good pilot.

Anakin's family and friends are
going to watch him race.

The pilots are on the starting line.
Ready, set,
Podrace!

The race is very exciting.
Sebulba does everything he can
to win.
He tries to push Anakin out
of the race.

Anakin is a better racer
than Sebulba.
Sebulba crashes!

Anakin wins the race.
Anakin's friends and family are
very happy, but Anakin is
happiest of all!

Glossary

Cockpit a space that a pilot sits in

Engines machines that make a vehicle move

Podracer a vehicle that flies close to the ground

Racetrack an oval piece of track that vehicles race on

Tools items that are used for mechanical work

Index